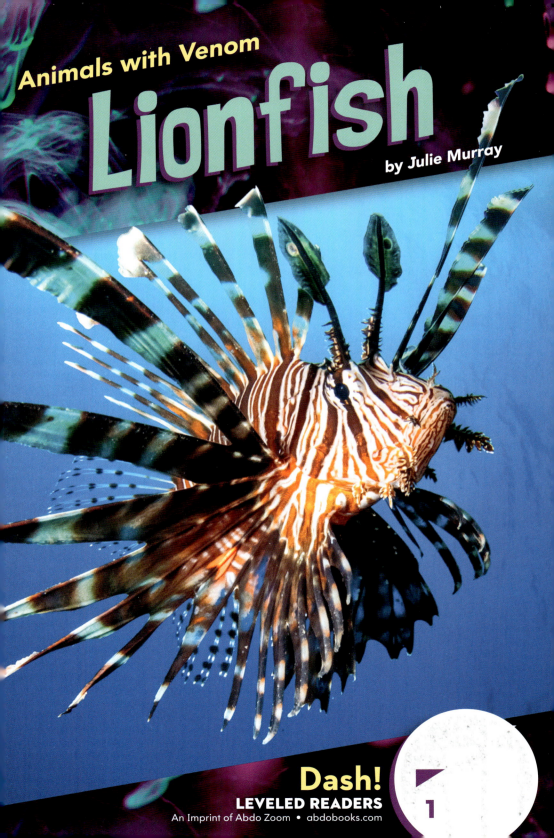

Animals with Venom
# Lionfish
by Julie Murray

Dash!
LEVELED READERS
1
An Imprint of Abdo Zoom • abdobooks.com

**Level 1 – Beginning**
Short and simple sentences with familiar words or patterns for children who are beginning to understand how letters and sounds go together.

**Level 2 – Emerging**
Longer words and sentences with more complex language patterns for readers who are practicing common words and letter sounds.

**Level 3 – Transitional**
More developed language and vocabulary for readers who are becoming more independent.

THIS BOOK CONTAINS RECYCLED MATERIALS

abdobooks.com

Published by Abdo Zoom, a division of ABDO, PO Box 398166, Minneapolis, Minnesota 55439. Copyright © 2021 by Abdo Consulting Group, Inc. International copyrights reserved in all countries. No part of this book may be reproduced in any form without written permission from the publisher. Dash!™ is a trademark and logo of Abdo Zoom.

Printed in the United States of America, North Mankato, Minnesota.
052020
092020

Photo Credits: Alamy, Blue Planet Archive, Getty Images, iStock, Minden Pictures, Shutterstock
Production Contributors: Kenny Abdo, Jennie Forsberg, Grace Hansen, John Hansen
Design Contributors: Dorothy Toth, Neil Klinepier, Candice Keimig

**Library of Congress Control Number: 2019956139**

**Publisher's Cataloging in Publication Data**

Names: Murray, Julie, author.
Title: Lionfish / by Julie Murray
Description: Minneapolis, Minnesota : Abdo Zoom, 2021 | Series: Animals with venom | Includes online resources and index.
Identifiers: ISBN 9781098221058 (lib. bdg.) | ISBN 9781644944004 (pbk.) | ISBN 9781098222031 (ebook) | ISBN 9781098222529 (Read-to-Me ebook)
Subjects: LCSH: Lionfish--Juvenile literature. | Dragonfish--Juvenile literature. | Poisonous animals--Juvenile literature. | Poisonous fishes--Venom--Juvenile literature. | Bites and stings--Juvenile literature.
Classification: DDC 591.69--dc23

# Table of Contents

Lionfish . . . . . . . . . . . . . . . . . . . 4

More Facts . . . . . . . . . . . . . . . . 22

Glossary . . . . . . . . . . . . . . . . . 23

Index . . . . . . . . . . . . . . . . . . . . 24

Online Resources . . . . . . . . . 24

# Lionfish

Lionfish mainly live in the Pacific Ocean. But they are found in other oceans too.

Lionfish live near **coral reefs**. They often hide in cracks in the rocks.

There are 12 different kinds of lionfish. The red lionfish is the biggest.

Lionfish are brown or reddish in color. They have white stripes.

Lionfish have feathery fins. They also have long **spines**. The spines contain **venom**!

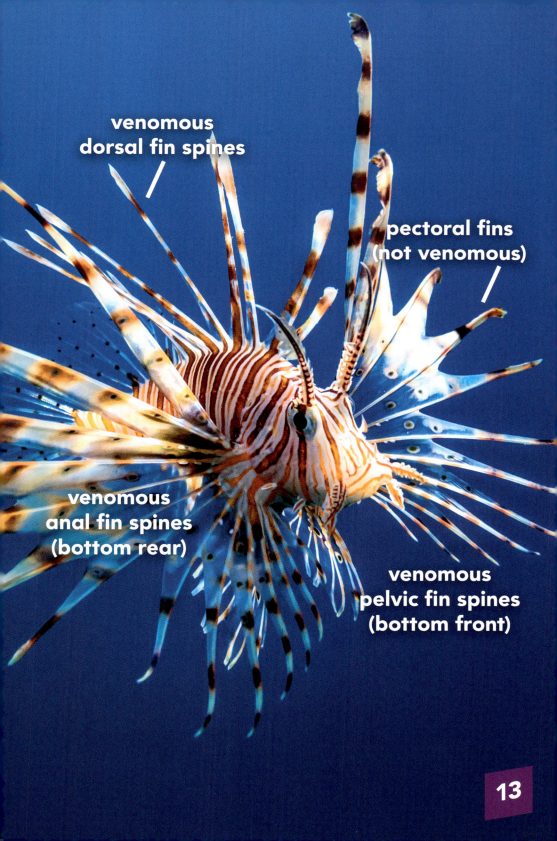

Lionfish do not use their **venom** to hunt. They use it to protect themselves.

A lionfish's **venom** is not deadly to humans. But it can make people sick.

Lionfish sneak up on their **prey**. They eat fish, shrimp, and crabs.

Lionfish spend most of their lives alone. They only come together to **mate**.

# More Facts

- Some lionfish only live for five years. Others can live for 15 years.

- Lionfish are kept as pet fish. They can't share a tank with small fish.

- Some people eat lionfish. The **spines** need to be cut off before the fish is cooked and eaten.

# Glossary

**coral reef** – large, underwater ecosystems made up of coral. Most commonly found in shallow, tropical waters.

**mate** – to come together to have young.

**prey** – an animal that is hunted and eaten by another animal.

**spines** – the needle-like bristles along the dorsal, pelvic, and anal fins that deliver venom.

**venom** – a poison that certain animals make.

# Index

color 11

fins 12

food 19

habitat 4, 6

hunting 19

markings 11

Pacific Ocean 4

red lionfish 8

reproducing 21

species 8

spines 12

venom 12, 15, 16

# Online Resources

To learn more about lionfish, please visit **abdobooklinks.com** or scan this QR code. These links are routinely monitored and updated to provide the most current information available.